A Guide to
AMERICAN STATES

Georgia

THE PEACH STATE

MEDIA ENHANCED BOOKS
AV2 BY WEIGL
ADDED VALUE • AUDIO VISUAL

www.av2books.com

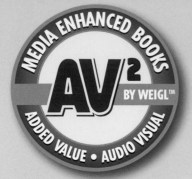

AV² provides enriched content that supplements and complements this book
Weigl's AV² books strive to create inspired learning and engage young minds
in a total learning experience.

Your AV² Media Enhanced books come alive with...

Audio
Listen to sections of
the book read aloud.

Key Words
Study vocabulary, and
complete a matching
word activity.

Go to **www.av2books.com**,
and enter this book's
unique code.

Video
Watch informative
video clips.

Quizzes
Test your knowledge.

BOOK CODE

N393138

Embedded Weblinks
Gain additional information
for research.

Slide Show
View images and
captions, and prepare
a presentation.

AV² by Weigl brings you media
enhanced books that support
active learning.

Try This!
Complete activities and
hands-on experiments.

... and much, much more!

Published by AV² by Weigl
350 5th Avenue, 59th Floor
New York, NY 10118
Website: www.av2books.com   www.weigl.com

Library of Congress Cataloging-in-Publication Data

Nault, Jennifer.
 Georgia / Jennifer Nault.
     p. cm. -- (A guide to American states)
 Includes index.
 ISBN 978-1-61690-782-2 (hardcover) -- ISBN 978-1-61690-458-6 (online)
 1. Georgia--Juvenile literature. I. Title.
 F286.3.N383 2011
 975.8--dc23
                            2011018322

Printed in the United States of America in North Mankato, Minnesota

052011
WEP180511

Project Coordinator Jordan McGill
Art Director Terry Paulhus

Photo Credits
Every reasonable effort has been made to trace ownership and to obtain permission to reprint copyright material. The publishers would be pleased to have any errors or omissions brought to their attention so that they may be corrected in subsequent printings.

Weigl acknowledges Getty Images as its primary image supplier for this title.

Contents

With a population of more than 540,000, Atlanta is both the state capital and Georgia's largest city.

Introduction

Two of Georgia's nicknames are the Peach State and the Empire State of the South. The first nickname stems from the fact that Georgia has long been one of the nation's leading peach producers. The second nickname refers to Georgia's role as the center of agricultural and industrial development in the South. The state was once the cotton capital of the nation, and cotton production is still one of its main industries.

The colony of Georgia was founded in 1733 and was named after Great Britain's King George II. Georgians were among the first to sign the Declaration of Independence in 1776. On January 2, 1788, Georgia became a state. It was the first Southern state to join the Union.

Cascading more than 60 feet, the scenic Minnehaha Falls attracts hikers to Rabun County, in northeast Georgia.

Georgia orchards produce more than 40 varieties of peaches, with most trees blossoming from mid-March to early April.

In Georgia's early years, the state's many cotton **plantations** prospered. The people who owned the plantations depended on the labor of African American slaves. Slavery was a major reason why Georgia sided with the Confederacy during the Civil War. Georgia suffered enormously in the war, and many Georgians were killed or imprisoned.

The Civil War ended slavery in Georgia, but African Americans then suffered for decades under **segregation**. This system kept African Americans separate from the rest of the population and prevented them from using the same public places, such as schools and restaurants. In the mid-20th century, the **civil rights movement** worked to gain equal rights for African Americans. Born and raised in Atlanta, Martin Luther King, Jr., was a leader in this movement.

Where Is Georgia?

Georgia is located in the Deep South of the United States. The southeastern corner of the state skims the Atlantic Ocean, with several islands located just offshore. Georgia is bordered by Florida to the south, Alabama to the west, Tennessee and North Carolina to the north, and South Carolina to the east.

From its main hub in Atlanta, Delta Air Lines offers about 1,000 flights a day to more than 200 different destinations.

Georgia has 1,244 miles of interstate highways, many of which intersect at Atlanta.

Georgia is home to more than 100 commercial airports, with the Hartsfield-Jackson Atlanta International Airport serving as the state's main hub. The Atlanta airport ranks among the busiest in the country and in the entire world.

Amtrak provides passenger rail service to Atlanta, Savannah, and other Georgia cities. Interstate 20, or I-20, is a major west-east highway, connecting Atlanta with Augusta, Georgia. Atlanta is also the main junction for I-85, which crosses the state from northeast to southwest, and I-75, which links Atlanta with Macon to the southeast.

I DIDN'T KNOW THAT!

The design of Georgia's state flag has changed repeatedly over time. The current flag is based on the first flag of the Confederate states during the Civil War, with the addition of the state coat of arms. The design was adopted on May 8, 2003.

The state motto, "Wisdom, Justice, and Moderation," has been in use since 1798.

Georgia was one of the original 13 British colonies in America. It was the fourth state to join the Union.

After Abraham Lincoln was elected president, Georgia declared itself a free republic and left the Union. Georgia was readmitted to the Union as a state in 1870.

Union soldiers set fire to Atlanta and destroyed the countryside in 1864 during the **March to the Sea**, led by Union General William Tecumseh Sherman.

Mapping Georgia

The total area of Georgia is 59,425 square miles. Land makes up 57,906 square miles, and water accounts for the remaining 1,519 square miles. Ranked by total area, Georgia is 24th in size among the 50 states. Georgia's shoreline extends more than 2,300 miles, including the outer coast, bays, islands, and the mouths of river and creeks.

Sites and Symbols

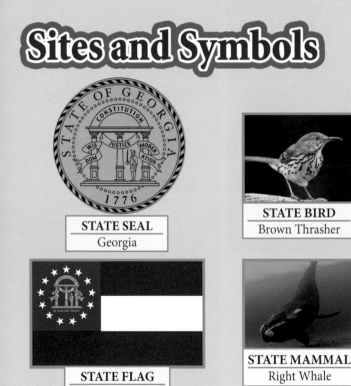

STATE SEAL
Georgia

STATE BIRD
Brown Thrasher

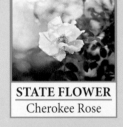

STATE FLOWER
Cherokee Rose

STATE FLAG
Georgia

STATE MAMMAL
Right Whale

STATE TREE
Live Oak

Nickname The Peach State

Motto "Wisdom, Justice, and Moderation"

Song "Georgia on My Mind," words by Stuart Gorrell and music by Hoagy Carmichael

Entered the Union January 2, 1788, as the 4th state

Capital Atlanta

Population (2010 Census) 9,687,653 Ranked 9th state

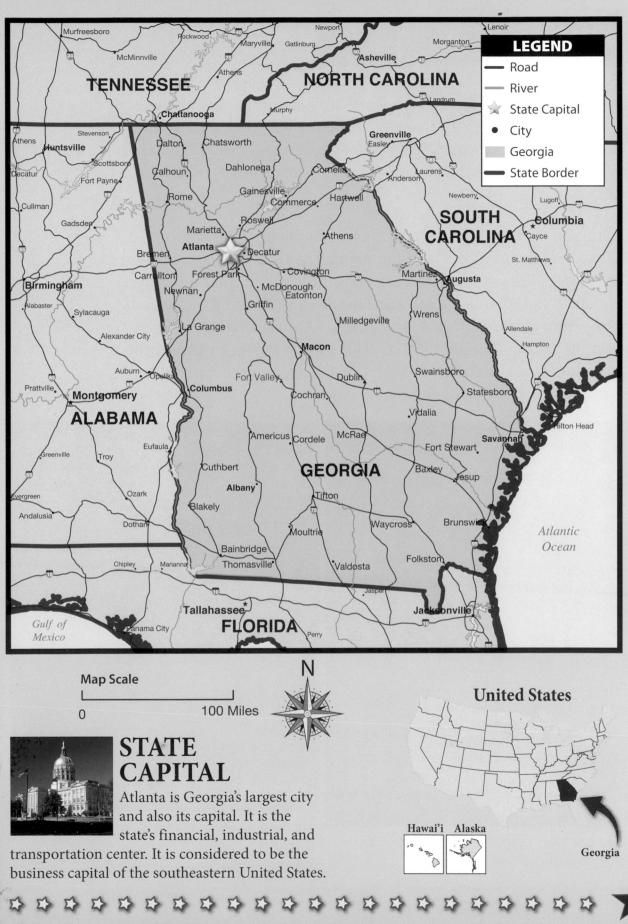

LEGEND

- —— Road
- —— River
- ⭐ State Capital
- • City
- ▨ Georgia
- —— State Border

TENNESSEE

NORTH CAROLINA

SOUTH CAROLINA

ALABAMA

GEORGIA

FLORIDA

Atlantic Ocean

Gulf of Mexico

Murfreesboro · McMinnville · Rockwood · Maryville · Newport · Gatlinburg · Lenoir · Morganton · Landrum
Athens · Chattanooga · Murphy · Asheville · Greenville · Easley · Anderson · Laurens · Newberry · Lugoff
Huntsville · Stevenson · Dalton · Chatsworth · Dahlonega · Cornelia · Hartwell · Columbia · Cayce
Decatur · Scottsboro · Fort Payne · Calhoun · Gainesville · Commerce · Athens · St. Matthews
Cullman · Rome · Roswell · Marietta · Decatur · Covington · Martinez · Augusta
Gadsden · Atlanta · Bremen · Carrollton · Forest Park · McDonough · Eatonton · Wrens · Allendale · Hampton
Birmingham · Newnan · Griffin · Milledgeville · Swainsboro
Alabaster · Sylacauga · La Grange · Macon · Fort Valley · Dublin · Statesboro
Alexander City · Auburn · Opelika · Columbus · Cochran · Vidalia · Savannah · Hilton Head
Prattville · Montgomery · Fort Valley · Americus · Cordele · McRae · Fort Stewart · Brunswick
Greenville · Troy · Eufaula · Cuthbert · Albany · Baxley · Jesup
Evergreen · Ozark · Blakely · Tifton · Waycross
Andalusia · Dothan · Moultrie · Valdosta · Folkston · Brunswick
Chipley · Marianna · Bainbridge · Thomasville · Jasper
Panama City · Tallahassee · Perry · Jacksonville

Map Scale

0 ——————— 100 Miles

N

United States

Hawai'i Alaska

Georgia

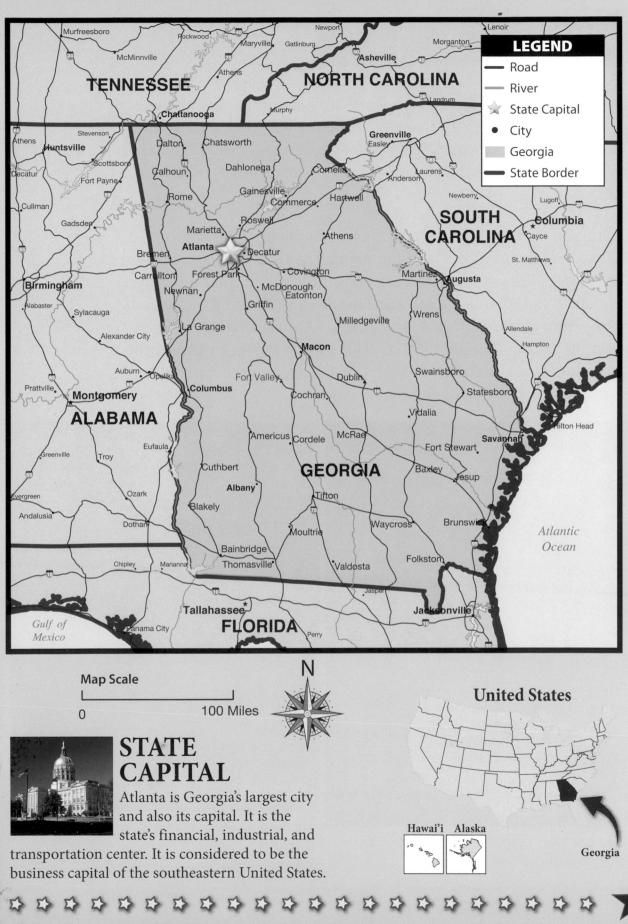

STATE CAPITAL

Atlanta is Georgia's largest city and also its capital. It is the state's financial, industrial, and transportation center. It is considered to be the business capital of the southeastern United States.

The Land

Georgia's landscape is a dramatic combination of swamplands, beaches, mountains, and plains. The state is decorated with moss-covered trees, colorful magnolias, and majestic pines. In fact, the expression "tall as a Georgia pine" came from the state's giant pine trees.

Georgia has three major regions: the Coastal Plain, the Piedmont Plateau, and the Appalachian Mountains. The Coastal Plain makes up about three-fifths of the state. It extends through the southern part of the state to the Atlantic Ocean and toward Florida, and it includes the swamplands of the southeast. The forested Appalachian Mountains are in the north. Between the Coastal Plain and the mountains is the Piedmont Plateau, a fertile, hilly area where most of the important cities and many of the state's farms are located.

COASTAL PLAIN

Live oak trees flourish in the Coastal Plain and on Georgia's offshore islands.

OKEFENOKEE SWAMP

The Okefenokee Swamp is home to more than 200 varieties of birds and at least 60 kinds of reptiles.

The Savannah River forms Georgia's eastern boundary with South Carolina. The Chattahoochee River forms part of the state's western boundary with Alabama.

Brasstown Bald, in the Blue Ridge region of the Appalachian Mountains, is the highest point in the state. Its elevation is 4,784 feet above sea level.

The official state seashell of Georgia is the knobbed whelk.

Most of Georgia's large lakes were created by damming rivers and streams. Major lakes include Clarks Hill Lake and Lakes George, Hartwell, Lanier, and Seminole. Located on the border between Georgia and South Carolina, Clarks Hill Lake is also known as Lake Strom Thurmond.

APPALACHIAN MOUNTAINS

The summit of Springer Mountain, in northern Georgia, marks the southern end of the Appalachian Trail.

SAVANNAH RIVER

The Savannah River extends 350 miles and passes through the city of Savannah on its way to the Atlantic Ocean.

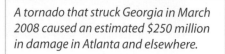

A tornado that struck Georgia in March 2008 caused an estimated $250 million in damage in Atlanta and elsewhere.

Climate

Georgia's southern location makes for mild winters, with snow rarely falling beyond the northern counties. Georgia's summers are usually hot and humid. In the summer the average temperature in Georgia ranges from 78° Fahrenheit in the northwest to 81° F in the southeast. January's average temperature in the southeast is 54° F, whereas the northwest dips down to 44° F.

Precipitation tends to be heaviest in the uplands of northern Georgia, and lightest in the interior region of the state. Tornadoes occur in the state, most often in late spring or early summer. Thunderstorms are common during the summer months, and the coastal region is vulnerable to tropical storms between June and November.

Average Annual Precipitation Across Georgia

The small city of Dahlonega is located only about 70 miles northeast of Atlanta, but it typically receives much more precipitation in a year than Atlanta and some other Georgia cities. What aspects of Georgia's landscape and climate patterns might account for this difference?

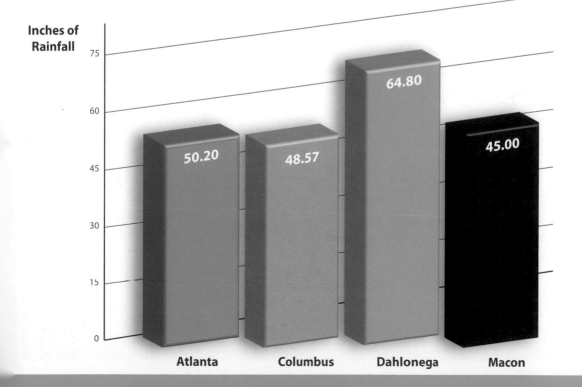

Inches of Rainfall

City	Inches
Atlanta	50.20
Columbus	48.57
Dahlonega	64.80
Macon	45.00

Natural Resources

Forests are one of Georgia's most important natural resources. More than 170,000 jobs in Georgia depend in some way on timber cutting and the processing of forest products. Georgia's trees provide various industries with raw materials. The state is a leader in the production of turpentine, a sticky liquid found in some cone-bearing trees. Turpentine is well known as a paint thinner, but it is also used in medicines. Georgia supplies a large amount of lumber and **pulpwood** to the nation. There are many pulp and paper mills scattered throughout the state.

Georgia has 24.2 million acres of timberland. More than 90 percent of this land is privately owned.

During the 19th century, Appling County, in southeastern Georgia, was known as the turpentine capital of the world.

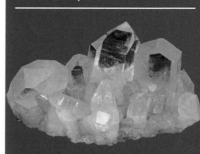

As a result of its large peanut industry, Georgia has earned the nickname the Goober State. In Georgia, "goober" is another word for "peanut."

Quartz was chosen as the official state gem in 1976. Quartz comes in a variety of colors and can be found throughout the state.

Pickens County in northern Georgia is the site of one of the world's largest deposits of marble. More than half of the monuments in Washington, D.C., are made from Pickens County marble.

Georgia chemist Charles H. Herty discovered a new use for Georgia pine trees. In the 1930s, he developed a way to make newsprint from fast-growing pines. Newsprint is the type of paper from which most newspapers are printed.

Georgia is an important source of stone and clay. The state supplies several types of clay, such as kaolin. These clays are removed from large open-pit mines. Clay is used to make paper, paint, plastic, and rubber. Marble and granite are both **quarried** in Georgia.

Plants

Forests take up about two-thirds of Georgia's total land area. Trees common to the state are birch, ash, sweet gum, sycamore, bald cypress, sassafras, cottonwood, and pine. Near the coast the undergrowth consists of shrubs, vines, and palmettos. These short plants thrive in the shade of larger trees. Palmettos grow well in sandy soils. In swampy areas, bald cypresses and tupelo gums are more commonly found.

Georgia's warm climate and fertile soils allow many kinds of flowers to flourish. Flowers native to Georgia include mayapple, bellwort, trillium, violet, daisy, Japanese honeysuckle, lady slipper, and hepatica. Floating lily pads and wild orchids grow in the fertile waters of the Okefenokee Swamp, located mostly in southeastern Georgia along the border with Florida. Thick Spanish moss covers the swamp's many cypress trees.

LILY PADS

Lily leaves, called pads, provide a habitat for small fish, insects, crayfish, and frogs.

AZALEAS

Georgia's many different azalea species bloom from March until August.

SPANISH MOSS

Spanish moss plants wind around the trunk and branches of bald cypresses and other trees. The moss lives on moisture and nutrients from the air and the leaves of host trees.

SAW PALMETTO

The saw palmetto grows in the Coastal Plain and produces sharp, saw-toothed leaves that are 2 to 3 feet long.

Georgia's state flower, the Cherokee rose, has a legend attached to it. Cherokee mothers wept when settlers forced them off their land. The legend claims that a rose grew wherever their tears had fallen.

Georgia's state wildflower is the azalea. This colorful flower can be found across the state.

The live oak, which is the state tree, prospers in the southern part of the Coastal Plain.

More than 20 plant species in the state are threatened or **endangered species**.

The Vidalia sweet onion became the official state vegetable in 1990.

Animals

There is a wide range of wildlife in Georgia. Animals of the forest include black bears, deer, flying squirrels, muskrats, foxes, and raccoons. In the south, alligators, turtles, crabs, and shrimps inhabit the coastal waters. Fish in Georgia's lakes and rivers include rainbow trout, shad, catfish, eel, and bass.

Many kinds of birds can be found in the state. **Game birds** include quail, ruffed grouse, marsh hens, ducks, and wild turkeys. Notable among Georgia's songbirds are wood thrushes, mockingbirds, and brown thrashers.

Human contact and natural predators have taken a toll on Georgia's wildlife. At least 20 animal species are listed as endangered in the state, including the right whale, the Florida panther, the red-cockaded woodpecker, and several types of turtle.

AMERICAN ALLIGATOR

Native to the state, the American alligator inhabits the rivers, ponds, and freshwater lakes of Georgia's Coastal Plain.

RED-COCKADED WOODPECKER

With help from the federal and state governments and local groups, the red-cockaded woodpecker population has begun to recover from near-extinction.

BLACK BEAR

Many of Georgia's black bears live in the northern mountains or in the Okefenokee Swamp.

RAINBOW TROUT

Introduced into Georgia's streams in the 1880s, rainbow trout can weigh 17 pounds or more.

The right whale is Georgia's state marine mammal. This endangered creature can grow up to 60 feet in length and is the only great whale that is native to Georgia's coastal waters.

The state insect is the honeybee. Georgia also has a state butterfly, the tiger swallowtail.

Most of the Okefenokee Swamp is now part of the Okefenokee National Wildlife Refuge. This protected area covers more than 600 square miles of land.

The state bird is the brown thrasher. This bird also lends its name to Georgia's professional hockey team, the Atlanta Thrashers.

Tourism

Visitors to Georgia can learn about Southern culture and history by exploring some of the state's many historic sites. The images of three Confederate leaders are carved into Stone Mountain near Atlanta. Other major attractions include Fort Pulaski and Andersonville National Historic Site, formerly a Confederate military prison.

Many travelers to Atlanta visit the Martin Luther King, Jr., National Historic Site, which honors the great civil rights leader. The Jimmy Carter Library and Museum, also in Atlanta, portrays the life and work of the nation's 39th president. The High Museum of Art is another popular destination.

Tourists also come to visit Georgia's beaches and seaside resorts. Some vacationers rent sailboats, sea kayaks, and other watercraft, allowing them to participate in a variety of water sports. Many people come to the state to fish for flounder, bass, and trout.

KING NATIONAL HISTORIC SITE

The Martin Luther King, Jr., National Historic Site in Atlanta includes the house where the civil rights leader was born in 1929.

FORT PULASKI

Built in the 1800s to guard the city of Savannah, Fort Pulaski was targeted by Union forces during the Civil War.

STONE MOUNTAIN

Towering 400 feet above the ground, the Confederate Memorial Carving at Stone Mountain honors Jefferson Davis, Robert E. Lee, and Thomas "Stonewall" Jackson.

HIGH MUSEUM OF ART

The American architect Richard Meier designed a stunning new home for Atlanta's High Museum of Art, which opened in 1983.

President Franklin D. Roosevelt kept a home in Georgia, called the Little White House. It was built for the president's use while he was taking treatments in the waters of nearby Warm Springs. The waters were believed to have healing powers.

Tourists spend more than $20 billion in the state per year.

The Kangaroo Conservation Center, near Atlanta, is home to more than 200 kangaroos, the largest group outside of Australia.

Industry

U ntil the early 1900s, Georgia's economy depended largely on cotton. Before the Civil War, African American slaves did the work in the fields, while white owners profited from their labor. When the Civil War ended slavery, the plantation system fell into decline. Cotton crops were ravaged in the 1920s by a beetle called the boll weevil. Although the weevil was eventually controlled, cotton growing never regained the importance it once had. Today, farming accounts for a relatively small share of the economy.

Industries in Georgia
Value of Goods and Services in Millions of Dollars

Today, farming contributes only about 1 percent of the total value of Georgia's goods and services. In what ways might a pie chart showing Georgia's economy in 1850 be different from a present-day chart? Why?

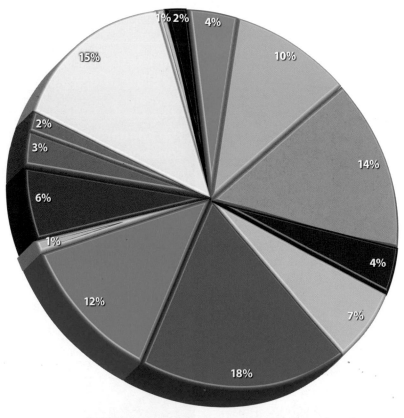

LEGEND

	Agriculture, Forestry, and Fishing	$3,499
*	Mining	$494
	Utilities	$8,924
	Construction	$16,482
	Manufacturing	$40,055
	Wholesale and Retail Trade	$53,577
	Transportation	$14,258
	Media and Entertainment	$28,443
	Finance, Insurance, and Real Estate	$72,670
	Professional and Technical Services	$48,211
	Education	$4,131
	Health Care	$25,672
	Hotels and Restaurants	$11,662
	Other Services	$9,376
	Government	$57,740
TOTAL		**$395,194**

*Less than 1%. Percentages may not add to 100 because of rounding.

Today, Georgia relies on industries that turn resources into finished products. **Textile** production is a major industry, and many textile mills experiment in making new kinds of fabrics for consumers. Commonly manufactured fabrics include velvet, denim, terry cloth, and corduroy. Carpet is another important textile product. Other items manufactured in the state include paper, automobiles, mobile homes, airplanes, processed foods, and chemicals.

A factory near Savannah processes natural gas from overseas. The gas is then sent through pipelines to Georgia homes and businesses.

Most of Georgia's electricity comes from the burning of fossil fuels. Nuclear power and **hydroelectric** plants supply the rest of the state's electricity.

Georgia's main exports include aircraft and other transportation equipment, computer and electronic products, and chemical products. Its chief imports include petroleum, iron, steel, chemicals, and food products.

Goods and Services

Georgia's farms produce corn, peanuts, pecans, and soybeans. Georgia has earned the nickname the Peach State for the quality and quantity of its peach crop. The state generally harvests more than 40,000 tons of peaches per year and ranks third in annual U.S. peach production behind California and South Carolina. The state's fertile soil is also responsible for producing many of the country's watermelons and cantaloupes.

One of the best-known Georgia products is a soft drink. In 1886, Dr. John S. Pemberton invented Coca-Cola in Atlanta. This world-renowned beverage was first sold out of a soda fountain in Jacob's Pharmacy. The name and logo were suggested by Dr. Pemberton's bookkeeper, Frank Robinson.

Georgia farmers harvest more than 3.5 million pounds of peanuts annually.

The Coca-Cola Company earns more than $30 billion per year from shipments of Coca-Cola and hundreds of other beverages.

Georgia's poultry industry has grown rapidly over the past few years. **Broiler chickens** and chicken eggs rank among the state's most valuable farm products.

Food processing is an important industry in Georgia. Processing plants freeze and can fruits, vegetables, and seafood.

Coca-Cola products are served in nearly every country on Earth. The Coca-Cola name and logo have become international symbols of American culture.

CNN is another Georgia-based company with a worldwide reputation. Founded in 1980, the Cable News Network has its main news center in Atlanta. CNN is part of the Turner Broadcasting System, which also includes the TBS and TNT cable channels and the Cartoon Network.

American Indians

Prehistoric peoples were living in the Georgia area more than 12,000 years ago. These hunters used shaved flint arrowheads to catch large prey. Because they hunted animals that moved from place to place, these peoples did not stay long in one area. Thousands of years passed before people started living in permanent settlements in the region.

The Woodland culture flourished in the area between 1000 BC and AD 900. The Woodland Indians developed agricultural skills that allowed them to settle in permanent villages, where crops and wild foods kept them fed when prey was scarce. These people are known as Mound Builders. The mounds they constructed were large, long hills made from clay and earth. Many mounds contained human remains, jewelry, figurines, and pottery. Some of the mounds were made in the shapes of animals. One of Georgia's many mounds is shaped like a large bird and is known as Rock Eagle. The Woodland peoples were followed by Indians of the Missisippian culture. The Mississippian Indians were farmers who used stone tools and had a highly developed social structure.

The ancient Rock Eagle Mound, built by Woodland Indians, is located in Putnam County and surrounded by a 1,500-acre park.

Cherokee and Creek Indians were living in the Georgia area when the first Europeans arrived in the mid-1500s. These Indians were skilled farmers, growing corn, beans, squash, and pumpkins. By the time the British made Georgia a colony in the 1700s, very few Cherokee and Creek remained. Many had died from diseases, such as smallpox and measles, brought by the first European explorers. Others had been killed by the Europeans or died while enslaved by them.

Between 1500 and 1700, at least half of the American Indians in the area died. In 1830, the U.S. Congress passed the Indian Removal Act, which forced the Cherokee to move out of Georgia to **reservations** west of the Mississippi River. The path that the Cherokee took from Georgia westward across the Mississippi River is called the Trail of Tears. About 4,000 people died on this forced march.

Creek leader Opothle Yoholo spoke out against the Indian Removal Act.

I DIDN'T KNOW THAT!

The Mound Builders were a highly developed culture. Their leaders, called chief priests, lived in temples on top of mounds made from earth. When a chief priest died, his temple would be toppled and buried under a layer of dirt. The next chief priest would then arrange to have a temple built on top of the buried one.

Ocmulgee National Monument preserves a record of some 12,000 years of human settlement in Georgia.

The Creek are believed to be direct **descendants** of the Mound Builders.

The New Echota Historic Site marks the former capital of the Cherokee Nation and the starting point of the journey west along the Trail of Tears.

James Edward Oglethorpe, the founder of the Georgia colony, showed honesty and respect in his dealings with Indians.

Explorers and Missionaries

Hernando de Soto was the first European to set foot in Georgia. This Spanish explorer arrived in 1540 and reached as far inland as the Appalachian Mountains. Several other expeditions followed in de Soto's tracks in the next two decades.

In the 1560s, the Spanish began establishing a string of forts and missions along the Georgia coast. The most important mission was Santa Catalina de Guale, on St. Catherines Island. The majority of the area's Spanish settlers were Franciscan missionaries who wanted to teach the Roman Catholic religion to the American Indians. The Franciscans built more than 30 missions in the region.

King Charles I claimed most of Georgia for England in 1629 as part of the colony of Carolina. The English arrived in South Carolina in 1670 and began expanding into the Spanish territory. By 1686, the English had gained control of the area with help from the American Indian population. Still, the English had to fight the Spanish for decades to keep Georgia.

Timeline of Settlement

Early Exploration and Settlement

1540 Spanish explorer Hernando de Soto becomes the first European to explore the interior of what is now Georgia.

1566–1568 Settlers from Spain establish a military outpost and mission located on St. Catherines Island.

1670s English settlers from the South Carolina region begin expanding into Georgia territory, disputing Spanish control.

Colonial Period

1733 The British establish the colony of Georgia, led by James Oglethorpe.

1750 A new law officially permits slavery in the colony.

American Revolution

1776 Georgia signs the Declaration of Independence. Patriots force the British royal governor of Georgia, James Wright, to flee.

1782 Years of warfare in the region end as the British evacuate Savannah. The next year, Britain officially recognizes American independence.

Statehood and Civil War

1788 Georgia ratifies the U.S. Constitution on January 2.

1838 The Cherokee are forced to leave Georgia along the Trail of Tears.

1861–1865 Georgia **secedes** from the Union and joins the Confederacy. The state suffers devastating military and economic losses during the Civil War. The Union victory brings an end to slavery.

Early Settlers

After the English took Georgia from Spain, many English settlers began moving to the area. King George II granted a charter to a British soldier, James Edward Oglethorpe, allowing him to start a colony for Britain's poor.

Map of Settlements and Resources in Early Georgia

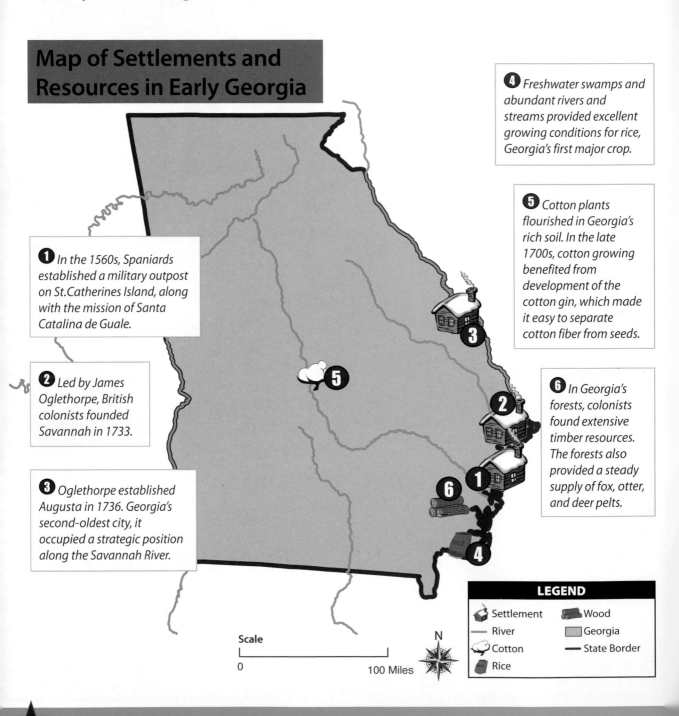

❹ *Freshwater swamps and abundant rivers and streams provided excellent growing conditions for rice, Georgia's first major crop.*

❺ *Cotton plants flourished in Georgia's rich soil. In the late 1700s, cotton growing benefited from development of the cotton gin, which made it easy to separate cotton fiber from seeds.*

❶ *In the 1560s, Spaniards established a military outpost on St.Catherines Island, along with the mission of Santa Catalina de Guale.*

❷ *Led by James Oglethorpe, British colonists founded Savannah in 1733.*

❻ *In Georgia's forests, colonists found extensive timber resources. The forests also provided a steady supply of fox, otter, and deer pelts.*

❸ *Oglethorpe established Augusta in 1736. Georgia's second-oldest city, it occupied a strategic position along the Savannah River.*

Scale

0   100 Miles

N

LEGEND

	Settlement		Wood
	River		Georgia
	Cotton		State Border
	Rice		

Oglethorpe planned to create a perfect society, where poor British citizens who owed money or faced prison terms could have a second chance. Oglethorpe's vision was of a land where no one was rich or poor. Male colonists who were sent to Georgia by the British government were given supplies and 50 acres of land. Those who were able to pay their own way were given 500 acres of land.

Many early settlers lived along the Savannah River. Some of the British who settled the region grew tobacco and cotton. Others made wine and silk and grew spices. These products were shipped back to Britain so that the British would not have to buy these goods from other countries. This system was called **mercantilism**.

A boom in cotton production led to a huge increase in the number of African American slaves in Georgia.

Notable People

Georgia's long list of distinguished citizens includes two Nobel Peace Prize winners, one an honored civil rights leader, the other a former U.S. president. The state has also been home to best-selling authors and recording artists, a record-shattering baseball slugger, a trailblazing American Indian leader, and one of the film world's brightest stars.

SEQUOYAH
(c. 1770–1840)

Born in the mountains of Tennessee, the Cherokee leader Sequoyah developed a special type of alphabet, called a syllabary, in the 1820s. He traveled among the Cherokee in Georgia and elsewhere, teaching his people to read and write. Because of Sequoyah, the Cherokee had their own written constitution and published books and newspapers in their own language.

MARGARET MITCHELL
(1900–1949)

Born in Atlanta, Margaret Mitchell wrote *Gone With the Wind*, which has sold more than 30 million copies since its first printing in 1936. This epic novel portrays Georgia during and after the Civil War. The film version of her book, starring Clark Gable and Vivien Leigh, won the Academy Award for best picture of 1939.

JIMMY CARTER
(1924–)

Jimmy Carter was born in Plains, Georgia, where his family owned a peanut warehouse. Campaigning as a moderate, he ran for governor in 1970 and defeated a leading defender of segregation. In 1976, he became the first native of Georgia to win election as U.S. president. He held office for one term, from 1977 to 1981. He was awarded the Nobel Peace Prize in 2002 for his work in support of human rights.

MARTIN LUTHER KING, JR.
(1929–1968)

Born and raised in Atlanta, Martin Luther King, Jr., became a leader in the movement to gain equal rights for African Americans. He delivered his inspiring "I Have a Dream" speech in Washington, D.C., in 1963. His life came to a tragic end in 1968, when he was gunned down in Memphis, Tennessee.

JULIA ROBERTS
(1967–)

One of Hollywood's highest-paid performers, Julia Roberts wanted to be a veterinarian when she was growing up. Instead, she left her home in Smyrna and began taking acting lessons in New York City. She had a starring role in the film *Erin Brockovich*, for which she won an Academy Award.

Henry Aaron (1934–) hit 755 home runs during his 23-year career in Major League Baseball. Born in Alabama, he began his major-league career in Wisconsin with the Milwaukee Braves and came to Atlanta when the Braves moved there in 1966. He retired after the 1976 season.

Usher (1978–) was born in Dallas, Texas, as Usher Raymond IV. He spent his teen years in Atlanta, where his singing and dancing gained an enthusiastic following. His album *Confessions*, released in 2004, has sold more than 20 million copies worldwide.

Population

According to the 2010 Census, Georgia had nearly 9.7 million people and ranked ninth in population among the 50 states. African Americans and people of European ancestry make up the largest portion of Georgia's population. Among those of European background are many people whose ancestors came from Ireland, Britain, or Germany.

By the Civil War, African Americans accounted for at least 44 percent of the state's population. This was the highest percentage of any state in the Deep South. Today, Georgia has many more African Americans than it had in 1860, but African Americans' share of the population has decreased to about 30 percent.

Georgia Population 1950–2010

Georgia nearly tripled in population between 1950 and 2010. What are some of the reasons for such rapid growth?

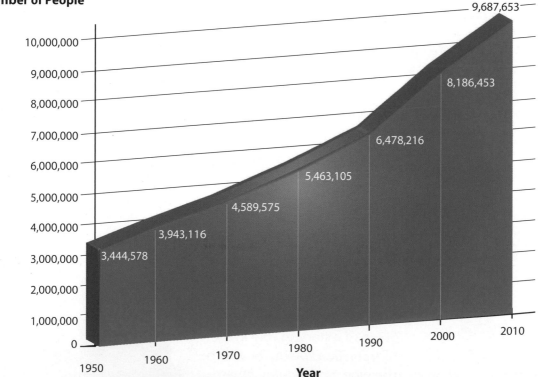

Founded in Atlanta in 1881 to educate African American women, Spelman College ranks among the nation's foremost liberal-arts colleges.

Georgia has fewer American Indians, Asian Americans, and Latinos than the national average, although the state's Hispanic population has grown rapidly in recent decades.

Nearly three-fourths of Georgia's citizens live in urban areas. More than half of the state's population lives in or around Atlanta. About 480,000 people live in the city, and nearly 4.8 million live in the wider area that includes surrounding towns and suburbs.

Today, Savannah is the center of a metropolitan region with a population of more than 340,000.

Completed in 1889, the Georgia state capitol building in Atlanta is a national historic landmark.

Politics and Government

Until recently, Georgia's citizens generally favored the Democratic Party. In fact, all of the state's governors were Democrats from 1872 until 1964. After 1964, the Republican Party became increasingly successful in the state. Newt Gingrich, a Republican from Georgia, held the high office of speaker of the U.S. House of Representatives from 1995 through 1998.

Georgia is divided into 159 counties, and boards of commissioners govern all but a few of them. Single elected commissioners govern the remaining counties. Once elected, commissioners serve their counties for four-year terms. Counties provide many local government services, including repairing roads and conducting elections.

Georgia's state government has three branches. The executive branch, which sees that laws are carried out, is headed by the state's governor. The governor is elected to a four-year term and also serves as director of the state budget. The legislative branch makes laws. The Georgia legislature, called the General Assembly, is made up of two parts, or chambers. One is the Senate, which has 56 members. The other is the House of Representatives, which has 180 members. The judicial branch includes the state's courts. The Georgia Supreme Court is the state's highest court.

Newt Gingrich represented a Georgia district for 20 years in the U.S. House of Representatives, becoming one of the nation's most powerful political leaders.

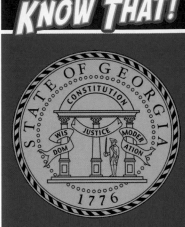

Cultural Groups

From visual art to gospel choirs, Georgia is rich in African American culture. Museums and galleries throughout the state keep the African American heritage alive. The Morton Theatre in Athens was an important stop on the African American entertainment circuit of the 1920s. Many blues and jazz greats played on its stage.

In 1968, Coretta Scott King established the King Center in Atlanta. The King Center honors the life and work of her husband, civil rights leader Martin Luther King, Jr. Visitors to the King Center include foreign leaders and international tourists, representing a variety of cultures and religions.

Coretta Scott King, the widow of Martin Luther King, Jr., helped keep his message of racial equality and nonviolence alive in the four decades after his death.

Born in Albany, Georgia, Ray Charles drew on African American gospel traditions in developing his soulful singing style.

More than 10 percent of all Georgians can trace their ancestry back to the Celtic culture of Ireland, Scotland, or Wales. The Theatre Gael in Atlanta promotes the plays, poetry, music, dance, and storytelling of Celtic culture. The theater gives Celtic Americans and others the chance to learn about Celtic tradition. Each year, Savannah celebrates its Irish heritage with one of the world's largest Saint Patrick's Day parades.

While American Indians make up only a small percentage of Georgia's current population, many events throughout the state celebrate their culture. Several annual gatherings feature displays on American Indian history, hunting techniques, tools and weapons, housing, and storytelling. American Indian dancers also perform and talk about the meanings behind their costumes and dances.

The Ocmulgee National Monument in Macon hosts an annual Indian Celebration featuring traditional dances, music, and storytelling.

The Tubman African American Museum in Macon celebrates African American art, history, and culture.

Many of Georgia's African Americans embrace the Baptist faith. More than half of Georgia's church members are Baptists.

The Albany Civil Rights Institute, which opened in 1998, tells the story of the struggle for equal rights in that southwestern Georgia city.

The Cherokee of Georgia hold an annual fall gathering in St. George.

The town of Helen honors its German culture with an annual Oktoberfest. This festival, held in October, is a celebration of German song, dance, and food.

Maynard Jackson was elected as Atlanta's first African American mayor in 1973.

Arts and Entertainment

Atlanta is Georgia's entertainment capital. The city's High Museum of Art at the Woodruff Arts Center displays paintings, photographs, and other works by internationally renowned artists. The Woodruff Arts Center also houses a professional theater and the Atlanta Symphony Orchestra. Clark Atlanta University has a long history of showing the work of talented African American artists.

Many of Georgia's traditional arts and crafts have their roots in the northern mountain region. Hiawassee and Tallulah Falls are famous for their art fairs and festivals. Many country fairs feature handiwork by local residents. People buy homemade blankets, weavings, and paintings produced in traditional styles.

Georgia has produced a number of prominent authors and poets, many of whom wrote about their home state. Among the Pulitzer Prize winners from the state are Margaret Mitchell, who won for her novel *Gone With the Wind*, and Alice Walker, who won for the novel *The Color Purple*. Poet Conrad Aiken also won a Pulitzer Prize. Short-story writer Flannery O'Connor is another well-known Georgian.

Born in Marietta, Travis Tritt has been a country music superstar for more than two decades.

Flannery O'Connor, a native of Savannah, was one of the most important writers to emerge from the South after World War II.

Georgia's long tradition of blues and country music has influenced generations of performers. Among Georgia's most famous musical artists are Ray Charles, Gladys Knight, Blind Willie McTell, Otis Redding, and Little Richard. The rock bands R.E.M. and the B-52s emerged from Athens. Atlanta's exciting hip-hop scene has produced artists such as OutKast, Ludacris, and Lil Jon.

In the field of modern country music, both Trisha Yearwood and Travis Tritt are natives of the state. In 1996, Yearwood had the honor of singing at the closing ceremonies for the Olympic Games in Atlanta.

The hip-hop duo OutKast had a huge crossover hit with "Hey Ya!"

Moviemaker Spike Lee was born in Atlanta. His early film *School Daze* portrayed student life at Atlanta's historically black colleges.

Comedian Jeff Foxworthy is a Georgia native. Other performers from the state have included Brittany Murphy and Stephen Dorff.

Blind Willie McTell was one of the great blues musicians of the early 1900s. He developed his own finger-picking style on the 12-string guitar.

Laurence Fishburne was born in Augusta. He starred in the *Matrix* series and other films and television programs.

Sports

One of Georgia's greatest sporting achievements was hosting the 1996 Summer Olympic Games. The Atlanta games featured an elaborate five-hour opening ceremony, which ended with boxing great Muhammad Ali lighting the Olympic flame. Atlanta was in the spotlight for two weeks while athletes from around the world competed for medals. The city of Atlanta spent nearly $1.7 billion on the Summer Olympics. Many athletes competed in Atlanta's majestic Olympic Stadium.

Georgia has five major-league professional sports teams. The Atlanta Falcons play in the National Football League, and the Atlanta Braves compete in Major League Baseball. The Atlanta Thrashers brought professional hockey to Atlanta beginning in the 1999–2000 season. The Atlanta Hawks represent Georgia in the National Basketball Association, and the Atlanta Dream in the Women's National Basketball Association.

Opening ceremonies at the 1996 Olympics in Atlanta honored the 100th anniversary of the modern summer games. Thousands of athletes from nearly 200 countries competed in the medal events.

The Atlanta Hawks play their home games at Philips Arena, which opened in 1999.

Atlanta's Olympic Stadium, renamed Turner Field in 1997, serves as home to the Braves. Over the years, the Braves moved from Boston to Milwaukee and then settled in Atlanta. In 1991 the Braves made history when they became the first team to reach the World Series only one year after having the worst record in the league.

Georgia has a variety of activities for outdoor enthusiasts. The ocean attracts swimmers and sailors, and the mountains draw climbers to their rocky peaks. Hikers, runners, and cyclists can visit a number of state parks and forests, including the Cohutta Wilderness Area in Chattahoochee National Forest.

Nature lovers can visit Georgia's 63 state parks and historic sites. Many of these have picnic areas, playgrounds, and cottages.

The Georgia Sports Hall of Fame honors great athletes who were born in Georgia or played for its teams. Hall of Fame members include baseball greats Henry Aaron and Ty Cobb.

In the early 1990s, Deion Sanders played baseball for the Atlanta Braves and football for the Atlanta Falcons. He is the only athlete to have played in both a World Series and a Super Bowl.

The annual Masters Golf Tournament is played in Augusta. It begins the first week of April.

On the Tour de Georgia, cyclists raced 600 miles in seven days while raising money for charity.

National Averages Comparison

T he United States is a federal republic, consisting of fifty states and the District of Columbia. Alaska and Hawai'i are the only non-contiguous, or non-touching, states in the nation. Today, the United States of America is the third-largest country in the world in population. The United States Census Bureau takes a census, or count of all the people, every ten years. It also regularly collects other kinds of data about the population and the economy. How does Georgia compare to the national average?

Comparison Chart

United States 2010 Census Data *	USA	Georgia
Admission to Union	NA	January 2, 1788
Land Area (in square miles)	3,537,438.44	57,906.14
Population Total	308,745,538	9,687,653
Population Density (people per square mile)	87.28	167.30
Population Percentage Change (April 1, 2000, to April 1, 2010)	9.7%	18.3%
White Persons (percent)	72.4%	59.7%
Black Persons (percent)	12.6%	30.5%
American Indian and Alaska Native Persons (percent)	0.9%	0.3%
Asian Persons (percent)	4.8%	3.2%
Native Hawaiian and Other Pacific Islander Persons (percent)	0.2%	0.1%
Some Other Race (percent)	6.2%	4.0%
Persons Reporting Two or More Races (percent)	2.9%	2.1%
Persons of Hispanic or Latino Origin (percent)	16.3%	8.8%
Not of Hispanic or Latino Origin (percent)	83.7%	91.2%
Median Household Income	$52,029	$50,834
Percentage of People Age 25 or Over Who Have Graduated from High School	80.4%	78.6%

*All figures are based on the 2010 United States Census, with the exception of the last two items. Percentages may not add to 100 because of rounding.

How to Improve My Community

Strong communities make strong states. Think about what features are important in your community. What do you value? Education? Health? Forests? Safety? Beautiful spaces? Government works to help citizens create ideal living conditions that are fair to all by providing services in communities. Consider what changes you could make in your community. How would they improve your state as a whole? Using this concept web as a guide, write a report that outlines the features you think are most important in your community and what improvements could be made. A strong state needs strong communities.

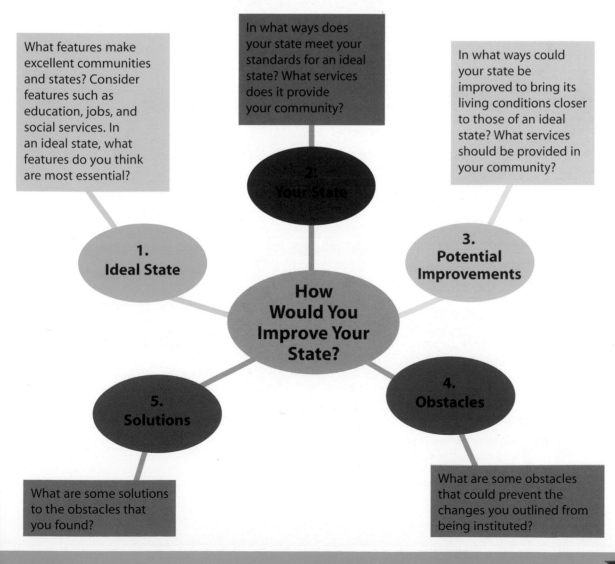

What features make excellent communities and states? Consider features such as education, jobs, and social services. In an ideal state, what features do you think are most essential?

In what ways does your state meet your standards for an ideal state? What services does it provide your community?

In what ways could your state be improved to bring its living conditions closer to those of an ideal state? What services should be provided in your community?

1. Ideal State

2. Your State

3. Potential Improvements

How Would You Improve Your State?

5. Solutions

4. Obstacles

What are some solutions to the obstacles that you found?

What are some obstacles that could prevent the changes you outlined from being instituted?

Exercise Your Mind!

Think about these questions and then use your research skills to find the answers and learn more fascinating facts about Georgia. A teacher, librarian, or parent may be able to help you locate the best sources to use in your research.

1 What is Georgia's most valuable crop?

a. hay
b. peanuts
c. cotton
d. corn

2 How did Blackbeard Island get its name?

3 Who was Mary Musgrove, and what did she do?

4 Why is there a tree that owns itself in Georgia?

5 What does the word Okefenokee in Okefenokee Swamp mean?

6 What Georgia city has produced a number of famous rock bands?

7 What important U.S. Supreme Court decision occurred in 1954?

8 What Georgia military site was named for a Polish immigrant?

Words to Know

broiler chickens: chickens raised for their meat rather than their eggs

civil rights movement: the struggle in the 1950s and 1960s to provide racial equality for African Americans

descendants: past relatives

endangered species: a kind of animal or plant that is in danger of completely dying out

game birds: wild birds hunted for food or sport

hydroelectric: describes electricity created from the power of moving water

March to the Sea: a military action during the Civil War when Union forces marched from Atlanta to Savannah, destroying the countryside as they went

mercantilism: a system to keep money in one's own country and its colonies

plantations: large estates or farms on which crops such as cotton are grown

pulpwood: soft wood used to make paper

quarried: removed from an excavation pit

reservations: lands set aside for American Indians

secedes: withdraws from a nation

segregation: forced separation and restrictions based on race

textile: fabric made by weaving or knitting

Index

Log on to www.av2books.com

AV² by Weigl brings you media enhanced books that support active learning. Go to www.av2books.com, and enter the special code found on page 2 of this book. You will gain access to enriched and enhanced content that supplements and complements this book. Content includes video, audio, web links, quizzes, a slide show, and activities.

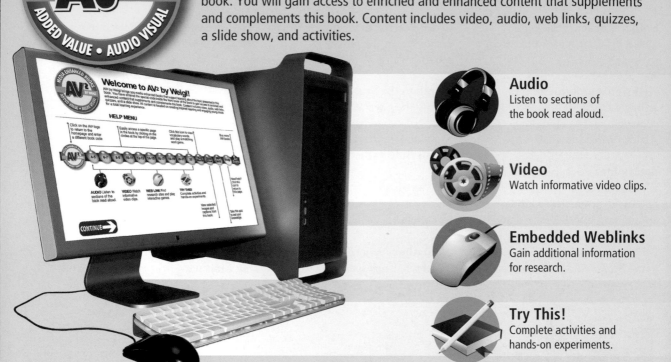

Audio
Listen to sections of the book read aloud.

Video
Watch informative video clips.

Embedded Weblinks
Gain additional information for research.

Try This!
Complete activities and hands-on experiments.

WHAT'S ONLINE?

Try This!	Embedded Weblinks	Video	EXTRA FEATURES
Test your knowledge of the state in a mapping activity.	Discover more attractions in Georgia.	Watch a video introduction to Georgia.	**Audio** Listen to sections of the book read aloud.
Find out more about precipitation in your city.	Learn more about the history of the state.	Watch a video about the features of the state.	**Key Words** Study vocabulary, and complete a matching word activity.
Plan what attractions you would like to visit in the state.	Learn the full lyrics of the state song.		
Learn more about the early natural resources of the state.			**Slide Show** View images and captions and prepare a presentation
Write a biography about a notable resident of Georgia.			
Complete an educational census activity.			**Quizzes** Test your knowledge.

AV² was built to bridge the gap between print and digital. We encourage you to tell us what you like and what you want to see in the future.

Sign up to be an AV² Ambassador at www.av2books.com/ambassador.